"The temptation to rein in ʲ   ... ᵣₑₚᵣₑₛₑₙₜₛ is premature. Turn him loose, let him play, watch him express himself on his own terms, and he'll lead you to a more soulful relationship with power, intuition, instinct and creativity."
Card #1, Field of Dreams. Linda Kohanov, Way of the Horse

"Horses are persistently hopeful that humanity will wake up"
Kate Solisti-Mattelon

"When we go to them and they walk away we should pause…..and consider….They may be saying "Where you are in this moment is not the right place. Follow me to a place closer to my world. It is there where I will show you how to heal"
Healing Horses 2013

Thank you to the horses and ponies who quietly and persistently invite us to join them in a different world…a better world, build on love, friendship and equality.

"Quality Time" Activities For You & Your Horse

Andree L Ralph

THE FREE SPIRIT PONIES PROJECT
Promoting positive horse guardianship based on friendship, trust, partnership and nature, through example and education

COPYRIGHT
The author asserts their copyright on this work (text and photographs). This work or any part of it may not be copied, reproduced or distributed without the prior written permission of the author.

ISBN: 978-1-326-05516-5

CONTENTS

INTRODUCTION

ABOUT ME

SECTION ONE: LEARNING ABOUT YOUR HORSE/PONY AS AN INDIVIDUAL

SECTION TWO: LEARNING THINGS TOGETHER

SECTION THREE: RELAXATION

SECTION FOUR: JUST ENJOY TIME TOGETHER!

FINDING FREE SPIRIT –
THE DREAM & HOPE OF THE FREE SPIRIT PONIES PROJECT

USEFUL WEBSITES, BOOKS AND INFORMATION

ABOUT ME….

I have loved horses all of my life but was only able to realize the dream of learning to ride at the age of 21 when I was working in a job that paid me a good enough salary. I still vividly remember those first lessons, learning how to rise in trot, surrounded by a group of 10 and 11 year olds who were happily cantering as if they'd been born on horseback!

I dreamt of owning a horse of my own but never thought it really possible. Then, around 2001, some devastating personal events proved to be a major turning point for me and before long I was working with horses every day and had bought my first pony, Stanley, a Connemara cross, who I still have and who has been my 'rock' and partner through many a down time.

Circumstances changed again and after much soul searching and logical, rational and calculated decision making (not easy for an emotional person like myself), I became the owner of six more wonderful ponies including a miniature Shetland, three New Forest ponies and two Welsh ponies. Suddenly my dream had come true in more ways than I could ever have imagined possible. However, that, I quickly realised, was only the start of the journey and over the last twelve years I have been constantly learning what it takes to become a true horsewoman in the eyes of my horses. The journey has pitted me against many of the long-upheld and traditional practices of horse-keeping and there have been times when I almost gave in and just did what everyone else did but my horses prevented me from doing that and I will be eternally grateful to them. We are now up to ten in the herd and have been able to include mares, including a 16.3hh TB – fortune worked her magic and found us a bigger field which meant we could offer a lifetime home to more horses/ponies and also create an environment that encouraged health and happiness.

Our horses and ponies live as a herd, outdoors, 24/7 without rugs (except in extreme circumstances) or shoes and are allowed to express their personalities and natural instincts in whichever way they chose. They share their field with a Kune Kune pig called Wilber and an abundance of wildlife and continually challenge me to be true to myself and what I've learnt. My goal is to share their 'magic' with others.

One of the things that used to really bother me about the horse world is that our horses and ponies are still seen as possessions or 'things' to enable us to take part in certain activities. For example, I am always being asked "What do you do with them (i.e. my ponies)?" For years, this really annoyed me because I found myself trying to 'make up' exciting things that I 'did' with my ponies so I didn't seem 'different'. Not any more though, now my answer is something like "I enjoy their time and company as friends and occasionally, we might go for a ride together". The expressions on people's faces are usually amusing as they struggle with what I've said and responses vary from "Oh…that's nice" to "Well I think it's cruel to not do anything with your horses". Not everyone but sadly most!

It was while mulling over another of these conversations that the idea for The Free Spirit Ponies project came to me. I realised that in reality I actually do a great deal with my ponies, none of which involves getting on their backs and the more I thought about it, the more the list of 'things' I did' grew longer! Every day I think of something else or try something else, so my list will keep growing as will, hopefully, my relationship with and understanding of my horses and the other animals around me.

This is a journey and I have no idea where the end will be or if there even is an ending (I hope not actually) but I plan to enjoy every step!

If you would like to follow the journey with us, have a look at and 'like' our page on Facebook – "The Free Spirit Ponies".

INTRODUCTION

Most of the time we just turn up at the yard, do the jobs we need to do, catch our horses, groom them, tack them and ride – why not become a bigger part of their lives, create a better bond and understanding and take some of the pressure of yourself!

All of the activities are designed to enable you to develop a much better relationship with your horse and are all based on the principle that our horses and ponies should be seen as friends and partners, not just vehicles or possessions.

This book is also written for horse owners whose horses and ponies may not be able to be ridden either temporarily or permanently for whatever reason or who chose not to ride, to enable both horse and owner to enjoy a fulfilling relationship, rather than feel frustrated and bored with the usual activities.

Some of the activities may seem obvious and the chances are you already do some. If you do, that's great – if not, why not try, you might surprise yourself and your horse!

Although in an ideal world all horses would live out in the open with a herd 'family' I know this isn't always the case, so the activities are designed so that many can be done either in the stable or while a horse is on box rest, in the field with other horses around, in the field or school alone or out and about. Some of the activities require equipment, most don't and some may require the help of another person at least initially.

The activities are divided into four sections:
LEARNING ABOUT YOUR HORSE/PONY AS AN INDIVIDUAL, LEARNING THINGS TOGETHER, RELAXATION and JUST ENJOY TIME TOGETHER.

I have <u>one</u> request when you are doing these activities with your horse. <u>Please - thank them</u> for their time and allowing you to be part of their world. It will be appreciated and will create an atmosphere of mutual respect, which is what this book is aimed at creating.

SECTION ONE:

LEARNING ABOUT YOUR HORSE/PONY AS AN INDIVIDUAL

The first part of this book is about truly getting to know your horse, physically, mentally, emotionally and psychologically. By taking the time to do this, your understanding of and relationship with your horse will improve a thousand-fold!

Ask yourself whether you actually know your horse and by this I mean, their personality, likes and dislikes, reactions to things, their normal physical health and appearance and how they communicate with you. There are thousands of text books and instruction books out there for 'looking after horses properly' and what to do if things happen or go wrong and every horse owner should make a point of keeping up to date with the latest research and information. However, as my partner is always saying (although in relation to fishing) our horses don't read the books!!

A horse is a horse just as a human is a human but in the same way as we are all individuals, which makes the scientific study of human psychology so elusive; our horses are all individuals too.

ACTIVITY - WATCH YOUR HORSES BEHAVIOUR AND LEARN WHAT'S NORMAL

There is so much you can learn by simply watching! Usually when we are at the yard, we are either busy doing 'chores' or preparing to ride. How often have you simply walked down to your horse's field and sat there and just watched? Or, if you stable your horse, spent time watching from a slight distance to see how your horse behaves? By doing this you will learn what is normal for your horse, after all, they are all different and what's 'normal behaviour' for one might indicate a problem for another.

I recently ran a short workshop on 21st century Horse-keeping (Natural Horse Keeping - Hark Hanson) and one of the participants suddenly realised while there that she had never just sat and watched her horse in the field – ever! Not even for 5 minutes. Although she took a great deal away from the workshop, that was the one thing she could change easily and quickly and something that will change her relationship with her horse for the better – guaranteed.

For example, I know that Whipper, one of my ponies, likes to spend time on his own, slightly away from the herd sometimes. He also likes to eat at 'one end of the row' rather than right in the middle of the group. This is normal for him. However, if Stanley were to do that I would be become very concerned as Stanley, being a rather dominant character, particularly at feed times (he was starved before I bought him), likes to be right at the heart of things in case he's missing out.

Red, one of my New Forest ponies and basically 'second in command' and the stabilizing force in the herd, much to Casper's annoyance, likes to hang back at feed and hay times and let everyone else sort themselves out before he ventures over. He is in no way submissive; he's just learnt that there's enough for everyone so why get caught up in the initial jostling when he can wait till it calms down and then wander over in his own time! Gizmo, on the other hand, also likes to be one of the first and if he hung back, again I'd be a little concerned that something was wrong.

This has been proved right on many a dark evening over the last few years! On one evening, Gizmo did not appear at the front with the others which immediately got me thinking. I discovered he had managed to get himself caught with one pair of legs on either side of a barb wire fence!! Fortunately for me, our herd are usually pretty sensible and have learnt to stand and wait when they are 'in trouble' so he had stood quietly even when the others came galloping for their tea and I was able to cut him free with minimal problems and no injuries. Another time he did not appear due to the fact that he'd escaped into next doors field and was happily grazing with their ponies! As you can tell, Gizmo does like to get himself into interesting situations from time to time!

Knowing what's normal for your horse can mean you have an 'early warning system' of illness, injury or other incidents, allowing you more time to deal with things sooner, more effectively and usually with less difficulties. Apart from anything else, standing and simply watching your horse from time to time is relaxing and makes you 'stop' for a moment which is never a bad thing.

Here are some questions you could start thinking about:
- What is your horse's normal relaxed body language?
- What do they do when they're excited?
- What excites them?
- What relaxes your horse?
- What's their favourite part of the field?
- Do they have a favourite friend?
- What are normal lumps and bumps for your horse? (You're going to have to get up close and personal to find this out!)
- What is your horse's favourite scratching spot on their body? This is such a useful thing to know as you can use this to build a better bond, calm your horse when they are anxious and reward them for doing something you've asked.

There are of course many more once you get going…….

ACTIVITY- OBSERVE WHERE YOUR HORSE FITS WITHIN HIS FIELD MATES

Finding out where your horses fits into their 'herd' is incredibly valuable as you can learn so much about their personality and how they deal with and manage relationships. This in turn, can then help you understand your relationship with your horse and where you horse feels YOU fit into their herd and they fit in with you. You can also discover how your horse solves problems or confrontations within their herd and how they behave around their friends and/or new experiences.

Many of us would love a horse that wants to be cuddled, that runs to us the minute it sees us and enjoys being fussed over. In reality, there aren't actually many horses like that – really. It's not because there's something wrong with them; it's just not what they do; it's not how they are.

When I first bought Stanley, I thought that was what I wanted too and for a long time, I would get upset that he didn't respond like that. It wasn't until he was able to become part of a stable herd and I was able to watch him within that herd that it all fell into place. Stanley is not an 'affectionate' horse. He never will be. He is a proud, independent, sometimes overly dominant pony, who isn't as brave and confident as he might initially seem. He will happily give up his leadership if another 'worthy' horse comes along but as far as Stanley is concerned these are few and far between and until he meets another one, he will continue to be in charge of his herd.

Having observed and realised this about him, my relationship with him changed for the better in all kinds of way. Firstly, I understood who he actually was and was able to accept him as such. Secondly, I was able to develop my relationship with him based on that knowledge and acceptance.

Stanley will take control in a situation if he believes he needs to - sometimes in a dominant way e.g. by walking 'over you' when being led and sometimes more passively e.g. by refusing to move at all or 'doing nothing'. However, given the right balance, Stanley is the greatest partner. By understanding this about him, I am able to match, adjust and monitor my behaviour and body language around him. When he 'leads' me, I don't punish him or get angry with him because all he is saying is that I'm not being clear enough or considerate enough and he is teaching me to be a better communicator. Once you develop this understanding, managing behaviour and dealing with everyday activities suddenly becomes very simple. There is no need to blame or get angry or stressed – just take a step back, look at what's going on and deal with it in a more productive way.

I have a herd of ten horses and ponies and they all have their own places within that herd. However, these places are not as rigid and linear as you might expect. It is not a case of horse A dominates horse B who dominates horse C and so on at all. The hierarchy is very dynamic and fluid and is very difficult to explain in a precise way, which is the case in reality with wild horses too. Herd dynamics are far more complicated than we first thought. For example, Whipper who initially may seem the 'outsider' and who is usually moved on by Stanley, Red and Casper can at other times be found sharing their food quite happily. Willow, who is what would be seen as fairly low ranking in the herd can at times be seen to be moving other higher ranking ponies around, and since we introduced the girls, occasionally even Stanley. Gizmo and Red seem to be able to interact with everyone and anyone at any time without (usually) being moved away.

I once sat in their field and had a chart in front of me to try to 'analyse' who was dominant over who, who was submissive and which ponies were close friends. I had worked out a whole 'tick box' categorising system and thought I was being very clever! Well, I sat there for half an hour and eventually gave up because for one thing, there were so many interactions between them that I couldn't keep up! I also quickly came to realise that many of these interactions didn't fit my nice little 'scientific' system! Initially I was a bit frustrated by that because I wanted to understand how my herd worked. After sulking for a few minutes about how they weren't 'playing ball with me', I realised that I had actually achieved what I'd set out to do i.e. understand my herd. I realised that it isn't about who can boss who around and who moves for who – it's something far more subtle and that each pony plays a part in a kind of 'dance' which enables the whole herd to thrive. Sometimes by being scientific, we oversimplify things to make them understandable instead of relishing the 'magic' and energy that they actually are. I have come to understand that herd dynamics are something to be 'felt' in the heart and not 'known' in the mind.

You may think at this point "well how can I understand where my horse fits with his herd mates then?". The answer is you need to observe all of the interactions and learn to recognise the subtle signals and body language between horses. However, when you are doing this, don't try to simplify it or create 'systems' as it won't work; instead try to learn to 'feel' what's going on and then use that new learning and feeling when you are interacting with your horse.

ACTIVITY - LEARN WHAT WORRIES OR SCARES YOUR HORSE

This is such a valuable thing to learn about your horse for several reasons. Firstly, if you know what worries and fears your horse has, you can help them and secondly, you can help yourself by not ending up in a situation with a terrified horse that you were not prepared for.

You can learn a lot about your horse's worries and fear simply by watching them as you spend time with them or when you're feeding, riding, mucking out, filling haynets etc. The more you observe, the more you will learn and the better you can make life for both of you! For example, I learnt the hard way that one of my New Forest ponies was scared of traffic (I later accepted that this was because I had not socialised him to it properly so the whole incident was my fault!). While playing, he had managed to jump into a neighbours field and I quite naively thought "OK, I'll just lead him back along the road and pop him back into his field with his friends". Unfortunately about half way along the road, a motorbike sped past us and Willow, my pony, lost all semblance of control and became completely instinctive – basically he ran!! He reared, spun 180 degrees, jumped over me, catching my shoulder as he did and went into a flat out gallop along the road, back to where we had come from where he proceeded to hurtle around my neighbours front garden at break-neck speeds! It all happened in seconds but I remember lying on the side of the road, watching his back end disappearing in a storm of hooves, mud and snorting, thinking "Please don't run into the road, please don't run into the road" and realising that my hands were now bleeding where I had tried to hang onto his lead-rope. Now you may think – well sometimes things just happen unpredictably or I should have done this or that. You would of course, be right on both counts, however, it could have been avoided if I had thought about properly training Willow for traffic earlier and not waited until a situation came up where we had to deal with it and neither of us were really ready. Often things happen when we are with our horses that are unexpected – it's life and there's nothing we can do to prevent it or control it. What we can do however, is prepare for it!

Every horse is an individual and although there will be some things that frighten or confuse nearly all horses instinctively, your horse will have thier own fears and concerns based on the experiences they have had so far in their life. By observing and testing (in a gentle, safe way) we can find out what these are and when they are likely to happen i.e. under what circumstances and start helping our horses learn to cope with these in a more sensible and thoughtful way. Part of the process involves building more trust with your horse, which is what all of these activities will help you do but mainly this is about planning for and preparing your horse to deal with these things and become habituated (used) to them in a respectful, positive and safe way at a time that suits and your horse – not when you're both anxious, stressed or scared and not thinking straight!

There are many ways to do this, some of which I don't agree with e.g. flooding (putting your horse in a frightening situation and keeping them there till they calm down) or negative reinforcement (pressure and release) when used aggressively. The main ways I use with my ponies include, where possible, placing the frightening things in their field so that they can learn it isn't frightening in their own time in their own way – usually this works a lot quicker than you might imagine as the only pressure they are under is the pressure they put themselves under and curiosity certainly plays a role with this method.

My ponies are not at all frightened by pigs, (see photograph) contrary to popular belief, as they live with them! They are a beautiful example of how instinctual fears can be overcome with time and patience and allowing the horses to 'work it out' in their own time. My ponies were not forced or pressured in any way to get used to pigs. They have over 12 acres of paddocks of which, the pigs pen is a small area, maybe 1/5 acre, in a corner. Initially they gave the area a wide birth (there was nothing they needed there) but as they had plenty of other space to be in, it didn't cause them any stress at all. Eventually over a period of time, they simply got closer and closer until now, as you can see, they have absolutely no concern about being nose to nose with one of the 'girls' (we had three when this photo was taken).

Something I have found really helpful for me is the fact that my ponies live together in stable herd and have done so for many years. I can guarantee that at least one of them will make the first move with something new or 'scary' in the field and will investigate and before long the others just get curious. The security they find in their herd allows them to be braver and take more risks and so new scary experiences are quickly overcome (in most cases) with this method and set-up.

I have used this for 'flappy things' by tying tarpaulins to trees so that they flap and make noise when it's windy. I have used it for getting used to new people, other animals, cars (by having a field next to a main road) – all kinds of things! Be creative and let your horses teach themselves its ok. When using this method, make sure that it's set up in such a way that your horse cannot scare itself more by getting caught up, running into something or similar.

The other method I use is positively working with my ponies, often in the field, to get them used to things like being handled for various reasons, saddles, rugs, whatever – again I use the safety and security of the herd to help them to stay calm and they have the option of running away if it gets too much. Everything is done in their own time and in a quiet, calm and non-threatening way. I want my ponies to be confident in me and in themselves so that if the unexpected happens and it will, they can make the decision to trust me and confront it thoughtfully rather than panic, possibly hurting themselves, me or others in the process.

There is no point hoping things won't happen or trying to avoid them because at some point, the thing you most dreaded will happen and it will be far worse if you haven't at least tried to help your horse and yourself work out what you might do when it does!

ACTIVITY - GET YOUR HORSES OPINION

Allow your horse to have a say and make some choices. Now you might think that's a ridiculous thing to suggest (you may not), however if you give your horse the opportunity, they will make their preferences perfectly obvious!

Most of my ponies don't wear rugs; they don't need them but Stanley has one sometimes if it's really wet and windy, (as does Sky, our TB). I have learnt over the years to 'ask' Stanley if he wants a rug on by watching his body language and expressions. He will be perfectly clear as long as I watch for the signs e.g. moving away, ears back and head swung towards me means "No thank you – I'm fine"! On the other hand, walking towards me, standing calmly and relaxed while I put it on means "Do you know, actually I wouldn't mind it on tonight". Interestingly, the more I have learnt to read his signals, the less I have put his rug on and he's doing better than ever.

When we rode more, I also asked him which saddle he prefered by either putting both on, one at a time and again watching his body language or placing both on the fence of the school and seeing which one he chooses – yes it may sound far-fetched but honestly it works.

When I put hay out for my ponies, I put some loose on the floor, some in haynets and some in my tractor tyre hay-feeders. Different members of my herd prefer to eat their hay in different ways and this can change on a daily basis but by doing this, they have a choice.

I don't own my horses and ponies so that I can ride. For me that's just a very small part of our relationship but I will also give the herd a choice in whether they want to be ridden too. If they don't, we do something else.

Getting your horses opinion and allowing them to make choices does not mean not doing the things that need to be done, or 'giving in' every time your horse 'disagrees' with you. What it does mean though is that you are establishing a two-way conversation which when done thoughtfully and with genuine consideration of your horses 'signals', can actually lead to your horse being far more comfortable with you making decisions when these are necessary and accepting the choices you make for them because they have come to understand that they can have a 'say' too. Remember your horse actually knows better than you how they feel and what they need and if we are willing to listen and if necessary negotiate, both you and your horse will benefit.

There are lots of areas in your horses life where you can offer them choices and these in some part will depend on what restrictions you have on where and how you keep you horse but by allowing choices, even small ones and 'asking' your horses opinion, your relationship will get stronger, become more equal and better for both of you.

ACTIVITY - LEARN TO COMMUNICATE WITH YOUR HORSE

The more you learn about horses, their psychology, their natural instincts, their abilities and their needs, the easier you will find it to communicate with them.

Horses are communicating with us all the time and we with them – it's just that a lot of the time, we 'talk' over them and don't stop to really listen!

Learning and watching your horse will allow you to learn their language and learn how they, as an individual communicate what they need to say.

I have spent time with many horses and ponies belonging to other people who are struggling because they don't know what's wrong with their horses or why they are behaving a certain way. Often with a little understanding, a whole lot of listening (with every sense I have, including my 'gut' feelings) and observing, the answer is very simple and very obvious – when you know what to look for.

One pony had back issues which presented as just a slight flinch at the withers when pinched – however, when properly investigated by a specialist, his whole neck was out of alignment hence bolting under saddle, another had just become very afraid and confused and simply needed to be reassured in a gentle, small way. Horses are generally stoical animals and will 'hide' pain instinctively as this makes them vulnerable so we need to be even more observant with our equine friends so that we can pick up on what's going on for them before they get to the point where they have to 'scream' at us.

With our herd we have developed ways with each one individually for them to 'tell' us what we need to know and you can do the same - you just have to 'ask' the right questions in the right way. Have a look at the section on visualisation too for some more ideas.

****

Taking the time to really think about who your horse is and who you are and of course, what you would like to be together is worthwhile in so many ways. Think long and hard about it. Do you really know your horse or pony? What do they like? Who are they? How would you describe them?

Think about your answers to these questions in two ways – firstly in terms of what it is to be a horse (physically, emotionally and psychologically), and secondly think about who they are to you in terms of being a friend, a unique individual. Take some time to think about this and if you find you're not actually sure take the time to find out e.g. how, when and where you horse likes to eat, drink, who they want to rest with and share time with? What noises and reactions interest, upset or frighten them? What do they love most? How do they react to you when you are with them, interacting with them or 'doing something to them'?

SECTION TWO:

LEARNING THINGS TOGETHER

This section covers some of the activities and skills that will prove invaluable for you in your daily contact with your horse. It isn't an exhaustive list but I'm hoping you'll get the idea! You will notice that I have not called these activities "teach you horse how to….". The simple fact is that our horses know how to do all of these things already and have done pretty much since the day they were born or very shortly afterwards. I don't mean that as a flippant comment at all – in reality, it's a simple fact. All horses can stand still, know how to lead and be led, can back up, pick up their feet, leg yield, half pass, lower their heads, jumps things and even piaffe and passage. All of the 'skills' are natural abilities for a horse. Watch a foal (or any horse for that matter) in a field with other horses and you will see most of these skills in a very short space of time. The problems occur when we as their 'owners' try to teach them how we think they should do it! On this basis, the activities have been titled "learn together how to…" as I feel that this better reflects the spirit, honesty and two-way 50/50 partnership with which these activities should be approached.

ACTIVITY - LEARN CLICKER TRAINING / POSITIVE REINFORCEMENT TOGETHER

….and then learn anything! Clicker training has been widely and successfully used in both the dog world and the dolphin world for many years but is still, as yet, relatively unheard of in the horse world. For me this a real shame as clicker training or positive reinforcement training is an amazingly valuable, fun and relatively easy method of training, which if done correctly and thoughtfully can change both yours and your horse's relationship forever.

There are many books and websites on clicker training/positive reinforcement training (Have a look at our Facebook page for some) so I will not go into great detail on the methodology here. However the basic principle is that you reward the behaviour (or a step towards the behaviour) that you want and ignore behaviour (as far as possible) you don't want.

Most horse training, including most Natural Horsemanship methods are based on punishment or negative reinforcement – both of which depend on the horse being uncomfortable in order to learn. Just for a second, in order to understand this concept, imagine you are back at school and have a test to pass, which you are not confident about. Your Teacher then tells you that if you fail, you will lose your new mobile phone permanently (punishment) and then says that you will not be allowed to leave the room until you have got it right (negative reinforcement i.e. pressure). How well do you think you would do on the test? Would you feel frightened, angry, under pressure?

Now consider, if you had that same test but your Teacher said if you did your best and tried the hardest you could, you would get 20 minutes extra break time (reward) and that as soon as you had done as much as you were able to you could finish (no pressure). How do you think you would do on the test now?

Take a few minutes to really imagine these two scenarios – really feel what both would be like. Now turn both into similar situations with your horse.

Imagine you want your horse to lead better. Traditional methods suggest that your horse should remain at or near your shoulder and keep pace with you until you say stop or whatever. Then traditional methods say, if your horse puts it's head down to nibble at a bit of grass, you should give a sharp tug on the lead-rope and make them walk on. Inevitably, what eventually happens is your horse will either 'learn it's lesson' or learn how to fight you – you have created a battle of wills and strength and it is really only by their generosity and a bit of luck that most horses decide to 'do what they are told' and not fight with us. However we have all seem many examples of when this goes wrong.

Using the positive reinforcement method, after building a positive, trusting and rewarding relationships with your horse, in the above scenario, you would ignore the horse sneaking a quick bite of grass but 'reward' them as soon as they took a step forward either with a tiny food reward or with praise, a stroke or whatever your horses loves most. By doing this you are systematically 'shaping' behaviour (yours and your horses) to a <u>mutually</u> beneficial outcome. In time, you will be able to negotiate 'that bit of grass' with your horse as part of the reward.

ACTIVITY - LEARN TOGETHER HOW TO ASK YOUR HORSE TO STAND

This is one of the simplest things a horse can do and yet seems to cause so many issues when we humans get involved! The photograph shows Whipper, one of my ponies 'standing' watching me and wondering what I'm up to. If you notice, he's actually standing pretty well square bar the front leg that's facing slightly towards me as he's looking this way! His back legs are square, his body is relaxed but his expression alert; his ears are forward and, as so highly sought after in the Dressage world, his poll is the highest point! Bar that front leg, it's an almost perfect 'text book' square halt! As far as Whipper's concerned however, he just stopped walking or grazing and looked to see what I was doing!!

Apart from 'halting' when ridden, there are many other times we need a horse to stand still / stand square and (usually) relax. Some examples include when tied up for grooming, the vet; the farrier/trimmer or at gates or other similar situations while being led.

Bear in mind, it is not a natural state for a horse to be in – being still – as they are constantly moving if allowed to be. Unless sleeping or resting, your horse would rather be moving as they are designed to do. Often people forget to teach their horses this fundamental skill and then wonder why they don't stand still when they need them to.

The simplest way to do this is to reward (a small treat or stroke) your horse when they do stand for whatever reason and say the word 'stand' followed by 'good boy/girl' or 'well done' or whichever wording you prefer. Very soon your horse will associate the word with the action and the reward and start offering to stand when you ask.

ACTIVITY – LEARN EVERYTHING ELSE!!

Once you have discovered positive reinforcement training (PRT) and got the hang of it, why not have a go at some of these too…..

- Spook proof your horse and yourself
- Learn together how to lead (again another skill that is often not taught properly or fully and then causes disagreements later)
- Learn together how to lead through gates
- Learn together how to ask your horse to back up
- Learn together how to ask you horse to pick their feet up and hold them there
- Learn together how to ask your horse to lower their head for you – for headcollars, bridles and general relaxation.
- Learn other lateral ground work together (leg yield, half pass, moving away, moving towards etc

Simply set up the situation so that your horse is able to offer a communication and try and then reward every slight step in the right direction. If you can do this at liberty the conversation will be much clearer.

It is ok to 'show' or 'direct' your horse if it's something they are unlikely to stumble upon by accident as long as you are guiding their actions in a positive way e.g. holding a treat/pointing to a treat down low to show that you would like them to lower their head. Choose words/names for things that you will easily remember and that are simple and clear for both you and your horse.

ACTIVITY - LEARN HORSE AGILITY TOGETHER

This is an incredibly interesting and relatively new activity with horses but is proving to be extremely successful and really helps to develop and strengthen a horse and guardian relationship.

Horse agility involves setting up effectively an obstacle course in a school, field or other suitable area and working with your horse around, over and under the obstacles from the ground – initially using a lead rope and head-collar but eventually, completely at liberty. When you get really good there are competitions you can enter (either 'in person' or virtually) and the ultimate level is at liberty, in a natural setting e.g. the woods, using natural obstacles!

Start off with something simple like walking from cone to cone and go from there......

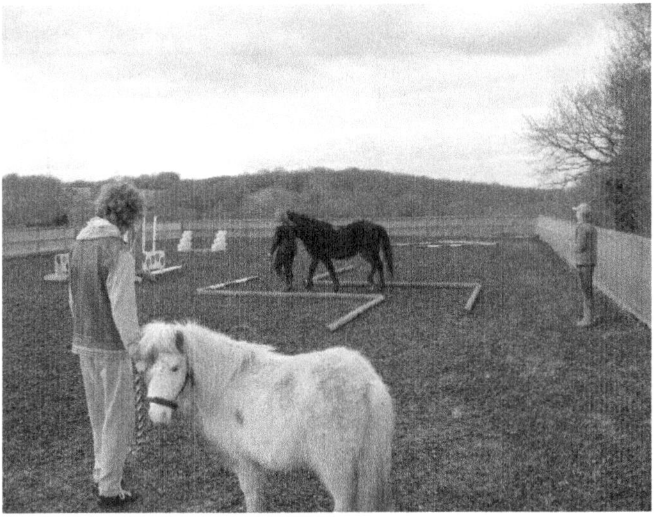

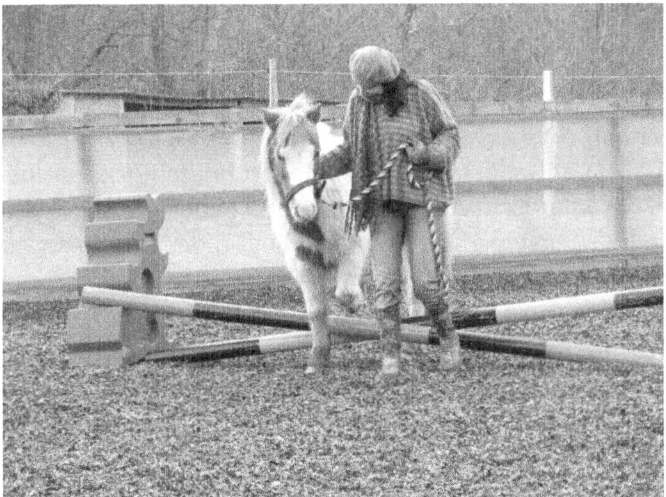

ACTIVITY - LEARN HOW TO FREE-SCHOOL TOGETHER

Free schooling is a very much under-rated activity, partly I think because it is misunderstood and inappropriately used a lot of the time. Free Schooling is not simply turning your horse or pony loose in a school or paddock and then 'chasing' them around so that they canter and gallop around the arena in a state of sheer panic and confusion! Unfortunately this is what is often done when people say they are 'free-schooling'. A Free schooling session should be a structured, thoughtfully designed, purposeful but fun period of time, spent with your horse at 'liberty'. It is about improving, enhancing and strengthening your relationship with your horse or pony not scaring the life out of them, while attempting to exhaust them. Properly designed free schooling will enable you to practice or even teach your horse potentially very complicated movements and exercises, without the encumbrance of tack and your weight, while ensuring that they are able to be relaxed and move in a way which is beneficial physically, emotionally and psychologically.

Imagine this scenario (unfortunately quite common):

Scenario One – You take you horse into the school and remove the headcollar and leadrope. You then pick up the riding crop or lunging whip you have bought with you and proceed to 'drive' your horse around the school in something resembling a cross between a 'spooked' canter-gallop and a confused, disjointed trot. To ensure you 'school' equally on both reins, at different points throughout the session, you stand in your horses path, doing a poor impression of a 'predator' leaping out from a bush so that your horse comes to a sliding stop and does a 360 spin before heading off just as frightened and confused in the other direction. After 20 minutes, you are exhausted, as is your horse and you are both sweating and breathing hard which surely means you have completed a successful free-schooling session….doesn't it?

Ok… let's have a look at another scenario (not so common but far more beautiful and emotional to watch):

Scenario Two – Having already established a respectful and balanced relationship with your horse and as part of an individually designed and fun exercise and 'schooling' programme, you lead your horse into the school and remove the headcollar and lead rope. For the first couple of minutes, you allow your horse to have a good look round, sniff and check out anything of interest or that might cause worry and even have a roll if they choose to. You have a good stretch yourself and ensure there aren't any 'dangers' left lying around in the school. After this initial 'relaxing' period for both of you, you ask your horse to come and join you, which they willingly do. For the next 20 minutes, together you work on stretching, extension and collection in walk through the use of body language and carefully designed exercises based on your horses natural way of carrying themselves, using your knowledge of horse psychology and communicating through positive reinforcement, imitation and demonstration to help your horse understand and learn what you are asking them to do. As always you find yourself laughing and smiling a lot and your horse's body language and vocal sounds suggests they are enjoying things too. At the end of the session, you signal to your horse to say 'thank you for an enjoyable time' and your horse shows his enjoyment and appreciation in his/her own way and then scoots off around the school bucking and kicking before having a nice dusty roll in the sand. Following a good all-over body shake, they stroll up to you for a quick nose rub and the two of you leave the schooling area and head back to the field where your horse eagerly but calmly leaves you to re-join his herd.

I know which session I would rather have just had….and also which session would have achieved the most.

Free-schooling when used effectively is a valuable activity for both and your horse, not least in building and cementing a solid relationship of trust and communication.

As with the other activities, start small and simple – work on asking your horse to follow you, stop, walk on and perhaps back up at liberty and then build from there. Make sure to reward every try and praise every success for you and your horse wholeheartedly.

ACTIVITY - SHARE YOUR HORSE

By this I don't necessarily mean in the 'traditional' sense of sharing ownership and care, I mean sharing the 'experience' and 'relationship' you have with your horse, with others around you.

When I was very young, we couldn't afford for me to have riding lessons and certainly not to own a horse, but it was something I dreamed of all the time. I don't know where it came from as no-one in my family are particularly 'horsey' despite all being complete animal lovers. All I remember is that I loved horses and everything about them. My Mum knew that and did everything she could to enable me to experience being around horses whenever she could. We would visit farms to 'pet' them and stop if we drove past fields with horses in, so that I could go and stroke them. My Mum even managed to get me a few rides on horses that belonged to friends of friends of friends. Each of those moments was like a dream come true and I still cherish those memories deeply.

Now that I have been lucky enough to have horses in my life full-time (my dreams come true in more ways than I could ever have imagined!) I make it a responsibility of mine to enable others to have that same experience if they want it.

There are so many children and adults alike who love horses and for whatever reasons, will never be as fortunate as we all are to be able to have their own. What we can do, however, is provide opportunities for those people to share time with ours. My ponies have given so many others some wonderful memories and I don't mean by enabling them to ride, although some do – I mean by spending time being cuddled, groomed, talked to, stroked, played with and generally 'fussed'. There is nothing more rewarding than seeing a child's (or adult's) face light up when they meet your horses and then watching while they interact and share mutual affection and joy.

Obviously, you need to be aware of your individual horse's personality and behaviour but if you are able to do this, you, your horses and the people who's lives you have touched will be changed forever, from the positivity this generates.

****

SECTION THREE:

RELAXATION

In my 9-5 life I work hard as I'm sure you do too. My 'day job' can be stressful at times as well as incredibly rewarding but ultimately can also take a lot out of me, emotionally, physically and psychologically.

No matter how hard things get or how stressful things become though, our horses and ponies get me through it.

We all have those days when you just don't want to have to deal with anything else going wrong or anyone else 'demanding' your time or something from you; the times when you think nothing else negative can happen and it does – it seems to be an unfortunate part of modern living. Without my ponies and the other animals in my life, there are certain times I'm not sure I would have made it through and certain situations and experiences that might just have broken me. This is in no way diminishing the love and support I have from my family and partner who I care deeply for and appreciate immensely but... there have been and are times when only the herd (and other animals) can bring me peace and keep me grounded.

Part of my problem is I cannot relax! I actually find relaxing uncomfortable! It's a simple fact. For whatever reason, as I've got older, my ability to stop, let things go and 'chill' for a bit seems to have disappeared. However, my horses and ponies and the time I spend with them everyday, outside in the fresh air, surrounded by nature, wind, rain or shine, make me relax in a way nothing else can. They also have an amazing knack of letting me know when I'm getting too stressed too but that's another story....

The following activities are about sharing time with your horse, doing things you might not normally think to do with them. However, by combining the two, you can re-discover a relaxed state of mind that you may have forgotten ever existed.

ACTIVITY - SIT WITH YOUR HORSE AND WATCH THE WORLD GO BY

With no agenda! This may sound easy but if you're anything like me, I can't sit still for more than a couple of minutes and especially when I'm at the yard or down the field. It's something I've really had to work at! I always had a tendency to find some little (or big) thing that needed doing and get up and go and do it – after all, when you have horses, there's always something to fix, prepare or do! There is also such pressure on our time in this fast-paced society, that we are conditioned to try to be as time-efficient as possible.

Most of us with horses also have to work (despite the common misconception that we are all rich) and have families and other responsibilities. We usually have huge pressures on our time and that includes the time we spend with our horses.

I used to look forward to time off of work so I could 'spend time with my boys and girls'. Then when the time came I would spend the whole week or whatever, fixing things, changing things that needed changing and generally doing all the odd jobs I hadn't been able to do. At the end of my holiday, I would be sitting back at my office desk feeling unfulfilled and frustrated that I hadn't actually spent time with my 'boys and girls'. Oh yes, I'd been there every day, I'd even been hours actually in the field with them but when I really sat and thought about, the only quality time I spent with them was perhaps a quick pat or stroke as I walked past fixing fencing or moving water butts. Not quite what I'd had in mind. So the cycle would start again – I'd look forward to the next period of annual leave so I could spend time with my 'boys and girls'! In order to break the cycle, I had to consciously work at it and it's not as easy as you might think. Have a go and see how many times, you get distracted by a job that needs doing!

I eventually managed to get to point where last Summer I consciously decided that I was going to spend one day sitting in the field, doing <u>nothing</u> except enjoying my horses' company. I packed a flask and some lunch and did it! I got some very strange looks from people I told about it afterwards but it was one of the most relaxing, rewarding and revitalizing days of my life. I learnt more in that one day about my horses than I had in years beforehand and I also experienced a true peace and calmness simply from being amongst nature and the animals that I loved with no expectations, agenda or plans.

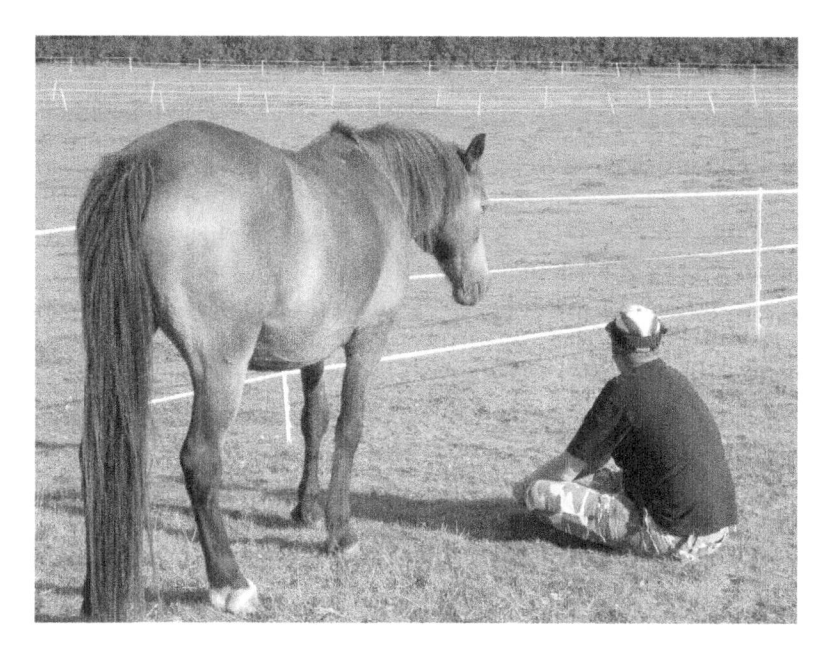

Of course, you don't have to do this for a whole day but even as little as five minutes every so often, can make a massive difference to your sense of well-being and your stress levels. Your horse will appreciate it too and soon understand that there will be times when you are there with them for no other reason than to be with them. Believe me when I say it will not go un-noticed and you will benefit from your horses' appreciation.

ACTIVITY – TALK TO YOUR HORSE

There are plenty of jokes about our horses being our therapists but the reality is they can be. There is a whole field of therapy and personal development that has grown from a horse's amazing abilities to teach us and help us see ourselves in a completely different way – a way that helps us grow and change and become the people we always could have and should have been.

Even on a small personal level, there are thousands of anecdotal stories from people whose horses have quite literally changed their lives or even saved their lives.

I think at a very simple level (and it's so much more in reality) the problems we often encounter in our everyday lives come from trying to play too many 'roles', not being true to ourselves, trying to 'compete' in a fast-paced competitive and sometimes unforgiving world and not talking to each other or sharing our worries and problems. This is where our horses can become our teachers. Simply by watching how your horses interacts with their friends and the environment, how they problem-solve, how they express themselves (if we are truly listening) and how they interact with us, we can reflect on ourselves and our lives and find similarities and ways forward. If you wanted to find out more about this important field of working with horses, have a look at equine assisted therapy and equine assisted personal development on the internet.

The one simple activity you can share with your horse, to begin to counteract some of the stresses and negativities of everyday life though, is to talk to them. Tell them your hopes and fears; tell them about your day, the highs and the lows; talk to them if you feel stressed or angry - they will know anyway, believe me, and by voicing it you will be releasing the emotion rather than carrying it around and pretending it's not there. If you have a problem or a difficult decision to make, tell them, share your thoughts – by doing so, you will probably realise that you have found the answer or know a way forward simply because you have bought things out into the open.

If you're really lucky and you really listen, you may even get the perfect advice in return!

ACTIVITY - READ TO YOUR HORSE

For a large number of us (myself included) reading can provide a great source of relaxation. Depending on our preferences, this could be reading fiction or non-fiction. If you find reading, in general, relaxing then why not try doing it with your horse?

This is an activity you could do sitting in the field while your horse grazes around you or near you, or while your horse is in their stable. The idea of this activity is to relax while spending time with your horse. You can choose to either read quietly to yourself or if you feel comfortable, read out loud to your horse – it's a great to practice doing this, especially if you are doing a presentation or need to speak in public because your horse will give you feedback using their body language and interest levels but certainly won't be critical or laugh if you mess the words up! Don't be surprised if your horse seems to respond to you reading, either by relaxing themselves, watching you or getting closer to you - either way, you will be creating a calm atmosphere for both you and your horse and you'll be enjoying some 'quality time' together.

I haven't actually tried reading books about horse management and training to my ponies yet possibly because I'm a little worried they might laugh! Who knows though?

ACTIVITY - BREATHE WITH YOUR HORSE

This activity is pretty simple and straightforward but can have real emotional and psychological benefits for you and your horse. Literally, stand near or touching your horse, whichever is most comfortable for you both and as the title suggests, simply try to tune your breathing in with theirs. You'll be amazed at how relaxing this can be. The other benefit of this is that you will be 'connecting' with your horse on a very basic level – after all breathing is fundamental to life – yours and your horse's. Again you may notice your horse relaxes as well and even drops their head slightly to doze. The key to this activity is not to 'force' it – just stand or sit and quietly focus on feeling the rhythmic movement of your horse's body and bring your breathing slowly in time with your horse. Just a couple of minutes doing this activity and you will feel relaxed, grounded and ready to carry on with your day.

Once you have practiced this standing still with your horse, it is also possible to use it as a technique for calming them (and yourself) down when they are a bit nervous or excited – I use this with our Casper often when we are leading as he tends to get excited sometimes, especially if we're leading towards the herd. I will literally say to him "ok Casp, breathe with me and we'll both get there quicker" and then I consciously breathe deeply and slowly and focus on sending this 'feeling' through the lead-rope (if I have one) and towards Casper – it really does work!

Once you are comfortable doing this, you can try learning to 'quieten your mind' and meditating with your horse – again both of these activities will help you and them.

This is what happens when we meditate (or simply sit quietly, in a relaxed state) in the field, close our eyes and allow our minds to focus only on the natural noises and feeling around us………

Go on…practice 'breathing' with your horse. Start when you are both relaxed, in the field or over the stable door – relax yourself and allow your body to become relaxed and simply breathe...slowly and calmly – focus on nothing if you can.

After a moment, continue breathing but observe your horse's reactions to you – are they interested? Are they relaxing? How are you feeling? Start with just a few minutes and of you want to, build up and make it a regular part of your interaction with your horse – especially before riding or undertaking an activity together. You are likely to find that even routine things become easier as you re both relaxed and 'in-tune' – you can even progress to practicing visualisation with your horse about what you are planning to ask them to do with you – for more about this, have a look at the section on practicing visualisation.

ACTIVITY - STROKE YOUR HORSE

This is one activity that most of us already do at some point or another. However, stroking should be far more a part of our routines than perhaps it is. Stroking is calming and reassuring for most horses and simulates a mother's lick from when they were a foal. It is also soothing for many people to 'stroke' an animal and there is plenty of research into the benefits to our well-being of stroking dogs and cats e.g. reduced stress, reduced heart rate and reduced blood pressure. The same applies for horses. The action of stroking an animal induces calm and the rhythmic nature of stroking 'slows us down'.

Every time I watch equestrian sport on TV, I get slightly annoyed by riders praising their horses with vigorous 'slaps' on the neck or shoulder. Try getting someone to do the same to you a few times and see whether you enjoy it – my guess is not really! Slapping at its best is more energizing than relaxing and at its worst can be annoying and potentially painful!

Next time you want to praise your horse – stroke them. They will appreciate it much more. Every so often too, when you have a few spare minutes, stroke your horse, if for no other reason than its good for both of you and will help build trust and a respectful, rewarding relationship!

ACTIVITY - PHOTOGRAPH YOUR HORSE

Often the only times we photograph our horses is at shows, when they tacked up or on 'special occasions'. If that's the only time you take photographs of your horse, then you're missing out on capturing some wonderful memories of your horses' everyday activities and daily life.

As a horse owner I have my phone on me 24/7 for emergencies (I'm sure you're probably the same!) but I also make sure that any phone I have, has a decent camera facility on it too. Obviously it's not the same quality as a 'proper' camera but I know if I took a decent camera with me everyday, either I'd forget to take it with me or it would get damaged or lost because I'd leave it in the field or run it over with a wheelbarrow or something! So my phone camera is a bit of a compromise but I've caught some amazing moments on it – things I would have missed or only been able to describe to people, if I hadn't had a camera with me. I don't know about you but sometimes a description just doesn't do things justice, where as a picture 'speaks a thousand words' as the saying goes! It also means that I have a nearly complete record of my horses' lives, through all the seasons of the year and through all of the up's and down's.

My partner recently bought me a small pocket sized camera which I think has actually become a great replacement for my phone camera.

I have beautiful photographs of my 'boys' in the Summer with their coats shining; in the Winter, either caked from head to foot in mud or wearing a 'snow coat'; galloping at full blast across the field; grazing happily with their 'best friends' or even flat out fast asleep! I have funny photographs (Casper stretching under the electric fence to reach a tiny tuft of grass in the next paddock or Toffee scratching his bottom on a tree), I have photographs like the one below, where as far as I was concerned I was taking a picture of one thing, only to find that what I had was something completely different – and in most cases better!

ACTIVITY - DRAW OR PAINT YOUR HORSE

You don't have to be a great artist, believe me, to gain something from spending time drawing or painting. That's why there is the ever increasing field of Art Therapy. When we were young most of us spent a great deal of time drawing, painting and scribbling. It encouraged us to be creative, allowed us to express ourselves and (as far as our parents might have been concerned) kept us occupied.

As we grow older and become adults, doodling and drawing become almost frowned upon and we are encouraged to be more controlled and focused. While these characteristics have their place, so do freedom of expression, creativity and yes, I'll say it again, having fun!

Next time you are going to spend some time with your horse, take you sketchpad and some pens and pencils and doodle while your there, Prop yourself against a tree and sketch your horse while they do whatever they're doing. Don't concentrate on details or getting it perfect, allow the pens to capture the freedom and spirit of your horse or the humour of a particular situation. Even if you only ever see these drawings and doodles yourself, their value will be immense in terms of the memories they hold and the emotions they will remind you of. You can even take this further by keeping a 'journal' of your sketches and doodles to 'carry' with you so you can feel and experience those emotions any time you want to.

ACTIVITY – VISUALISE WITH YOUR HORSE

This could have also gone in the 'Learning things....' Section but I decided to keep it here so that it is something that you can learn together to do but without the pressure of it being a 'lesson' as such. Visualisation can be used for so many things – to help us run through something in our minds, to evaluate and reflect on something that's happened and to 'create' a positive image/memory of something but it is also a wonderful way to communicate with your horse and share dreams together in a very relaxed way too.

For those who have never tried visualisation, it is a very simple exercise to do – getting it right (i.e. keeping it positive) takes practice but can lead to a very powerful and liberating way of working together and spending time together.

It is believed that horses (and most animals) see in pictures. Many humans do too – I know I am one. Visualisation with your horse works within this to build pictures in both your minds (yours initially) of situations, circumstances, events, activities, moments in time....whatever is most appropriate at the time. So for example, it is often used with those who may be apprehensive about jumping and find that nerves get the better of them. What they would do, usually with the help of a trainer is visualise i.e. picture doing the course successfully, making sure to build into the picture, the sounds, smells, colours and feeling that would go with it so that they are almost creating a future memory. They would then run through this 'memory' in their minds in as much detail as possible as many times as they could before actually jumping. What happens then is that when the person attempts the course of jumps, it feels like they have done it so many times successfully already, they simply get on with it and effectively 'copy' the memory they already have. It's a bit like mind over matter I guess. Believe me it works for all kinds of things and not just horse-related ones!

There are other ways this can be used and it's something I've tried on several occasions – for example try calling your horse from the field or asking them to come to you by picturing them walking towards you, standing beside you or in front of you quietly and contentedly and then 'send' that picture to your horse. Don't be surprised when they come to you just as if you had called them out loud – it may not happen every time but the more you practice, the easier this way of communicating will become and the more successful it will be. Go on try it…….

You can experiment with this, just always keep it positive and from a position of love and calm. After time you may find that your horse starts to send you pictures back of things they'd to do or how they would like things done too……

****

So, make a date with your horse to simply spend time with them to help you both relax and enjoy each other's company in a whole new way! Sit, stand, read, talk, listen…whatever takes your fancy but do it with your horse and allow them to be part of what you're doing……make a mental note of your horses reactions to you, what they do around you, whether they join you or stay away and what feelings and thoughts you are having – all of these will help you to 'know' and 'see; your horse for who they are and who you are together. The next section has some ideas for other activities you can share that mean you just spend time together too.

SECTION FOUR:

JUST ENJOY TIME TOGETHER!

There is a sense that when we are with our horses, the time should always be focused on achieving something e.g. schooling, working. There is so much that can be gained from simply spending time with your horse or even doing some of things you might normally but with no 'agenda' in mind.

ACTIVITY - GO FOR A WALK

No, this isn't on their backs – this is side by side. Go for a walk around the paddock, fields or local lanes. Depending on where you go, you can either do this with your horse on a headcollar or not. Obviously if you are out on the roads, the right equipment is a MUST including Hi-Viz and appropriate equipment for ensuring the safety of your horse, you and others as you would if you went for a hack. However if you are 'having a walk' around the yard or your horses field and it is safe to do so, you may like to try doing it without a headcollar. This way you can see how strong your relationship is with your horse and together come up with ways to help improve that.

I once took my Welsh Sec A X, Whipper, out to the local café and back to 'test' how road proof he was. His 'roadworthiness' was excellent – his sandwich stealing skills turned out to be much better!!

If you prepare properly and ensure you are safe and capable, this is a great way to introduce horses to new sights and sounds either in the field, the school or out and about. Practice 'at home' first though and develop the trust between you. By leading /walking with your horse, you are there where they can see you, you can take the first step towards something 'scary' to show your horse it's ok and you will be practicing your leading skills at the same time.

ACTIVITY - GROOM YOUR HORSE

It might come as a bit of a surprise that this one is in here as you are probably thinking this is something I do all the time! The reason it is in this section though is that grooming your horse has very valuable benefits to your relationship with your horse, in addition to simply getting them 'clean'.

If you watch an established group of horses (and often even in groups where the horses are new to each other), you will see horses and ponies 'mutually grooming' each other. Aside from the obvious purpose of scratching the places a horse can't reach for itself, this activity helps to establish and maintain relationships between horses and negotiate or confirm security within the herd. By grooming your horse, you are effectively doing the same thing or having the same conversation.

ACTIVITY - LEARN HOW TO MASSAGE YOUR HORSE

In some ways this follows on from grooming. There are lots of resources about to teach you how to massage your horse and lots of specialists that could demonstrate too. In its simplest form however, just a gentle 'needing action' on soft areas or a fingertip rub could see your horse melting into your hands in a similar way as we humans do!

This is an activity where it will help to know which bits your horse enjoys being scratched, stroked and touched and which bits they don't as you can include a gentle massaging action into the routine.

ACTIVITY - HAVE A CUDDLE

When I feel a bit down or upset or if I've had a tough day or sometimes just simply because I feel like it, I have Toffee cuddles!

No, this doesn't involve me surrounding myself in chewy sweets as the name might suggest! I am not a 'cuddly' person by nature with people but sometimes there is nothing more perfect than a cuddle with your horse.

Toffee is my miniature Shetland and absolutely loves being fussed, stroked, groomed and above all, cuddled. A cuddle with Toffee is like snuggling with a big fluffy teddy bear, especially during the winter when he has his winter coat, and does wonders for improving your mood. It has that same reassuring, relaxing and soothing effect that our favourite cuddly toy did when we were young. Obviously this will depend on the horse and whether this is something they like to. It would totally negate the benefit if you forced a horse who didn't like to be cuddled into being that close and in their eyes, restrained by you.

Years ago, when I was learning to ride, the pony that I rode all the time became pregnant (which I was very excited about). Unfortunately while she was out in the field one day, she was kicked quite badly by another horse and there was a short period when her owners thought that she may have to be put to sleep as it was so bad! Suffice it to say, I was devastated. During that period she was turned out on her own in a small paddock next to the school, and when I arrived for my lesson, I asked if it was ok to go in with her and see how she was. She walked straight over to me for a stroke and before long, we were both standing close together, her head on my shoulder and my head resting against hers cuddling each other. We stood like that for a long time (in fact, I have a feeling I didn't have my lesson that day at all) and it seems it was exactly what both of us needed! After what seemed like hours, we both breathed a long sigh, she wandered off to graze and I went home, feeling much better. She went on to have a healthy foal and continued to teach people to ride (including myself) for many years to come.

…..the moral of this story? Sometimes, everyone needs a cuddle and it can be the best medicine in the world!

ACTIVITY – 'CARROT' STRETCHES

I'm not the person who designed or named this activity but I know it's a fun activity and that usually you would use carrots as the encouragement! Quite simply this is asking your horse to stretch, bend, and use their body in different ways to reach a carrot or reward (treat). The most common 'stretches' are asking your horse to bring their heads either to the side by bending their necks or stretching across the back by bringing their heads down between their legs. This can be really useful for horses to learn to stretch and improve flexibility and you can use whatever stretches suit your horse, any injuries they have and what you need to work on.

ACTIVITY - PLAY WITH YOUR HORSE

We play with our dogs, our cats even our rabbits and guinea pigs and (usually) it is simply about spending time with them and having fun. Often it is a spontaneous activity that 'just happens' and both parties have a great time!

Why then don't we 'play' with our horses in the same way?

Of course, some of us do but most horse owners have strangely got a mindset that when we are with our horses, we or they must be 'working'. Even the words we use to describe our time together back this up e.g. schooling, training, etc. How often do you just go and 'play' with your horse?

Horses play with each other, if given the opportunity, a great deal of the time. Often this is mistaken for fighting (and among stallions and geldings particularly is likely genetically designed to 'practice' those skills) however, it is play behaviour and fulfils a number of functions including stress relief and exercise.

There is a sense of fear about playing with horses as they are so much bigger and stronger than us and do tend to play quite roughly – that shouldn't mean though that we don't interact with our horse in this way. It simply means we need to be aware of the risks (as with any activity) and organise things in a way that those dangers are minimised.

Now I wouldn't suggest you immediately go running out into your horses field and start encouraging them to gallop round with you, kicking and spinning (although how amazing would that actually be!). I also don't suggest you get your horse to roll over so you can rub it's belly. That's for your dogs (or Wilber, my pig!). Keep things simple and next time you are in the school or in your horses field, try playing a sedate game of 'tag' by asking your horse to come to you and 'tag' you (give them a small reward when they do), you could even build this up to a game of hide and seek, who knows – go with what works between you and our horse and what happens naturally. The idea is that this 'time' together is not focused on teaching, training or working – it's about having fun! There should be no agenda except enjoyment for both of you.

Ironically, as our horses don't actually differentiate between a 'playtime' and a 'lesson', especially if you have been using Positive Reinforcement Training you will probably teach and learn much more in these sessions, no matter how short, than you do in some of your pre-designed teaching sessions. The difference is more in your mind-set about the purpose of the time and how relaxed as opposed to target focused you are and that's why this activity is best suited to this section of this book.

ACTIVITY – DANCE WITH YOUR HORSE

Yes, I do mean dance with your horse. When we dance we are encouraging our bodies to relax and move fluidly and smoothly. We are also asking our muscles and limbs to stretch and find balance. Depending on the type of dance we choose to perform, a different 'energy' will be created and that energy will be sensed by your horse. You may find that they have favourite 'dances' or that different horses like you dancing with them in different ways.

Start by doing what you feel is comfortable – perhaps think about your favourite bit of music and simply stand in the field with your horse, or close to them and start moving in time with the music. Then, simply watch what happens and respond accordingly. Just 'go with the flow'. You might want to do this when no one's around if you're not feeling brave enough to 'boogie' with your horse in public!

Bear in mind that the more energy in your movements, the larger and more energetic, the possible reaction from your horse so you might want to start slow and gentle while you tune into each other and learn how to dance together safely and in partnership.

Here are a couple of picture of me and Willow and Darren and Flash, both starting a dance with our respective horses.

ACTIVITY - GIVE YOUR HORSE A QUICK PRACTICAL WINTER 'MAKE-OVER'

By this I don't mean bathing, plaiting, clipping, hogging or any of the other terms we use to make our horses look 'perfect' for the show-ring or when we are out riding. What I mean here is practical care. This activity is more suited to horses that live out all year and allowed to develop natural coats, manes and tails etc.

My ponies live out 24/7 all year round, mostly without rugs or excessive grooming. They grow thick, hairy coats and long manes and tails. Every year, usually during the late Autumn, I give them what I call their Winter 'make-over'. This isn't about making them look beautiful and grooming them till they shine; it's about doing a couple of things to enable them to get through the Winter without getting too tangled or being unable to groom themselves as they need and want to.

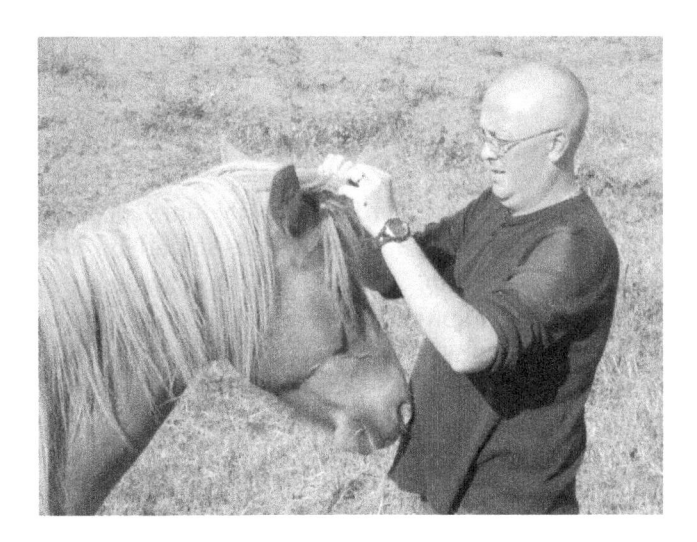

Each pony has their tail trimmed so that it won't drag in the inevitable mud and get 'nasty'. Their manes are trimmed slightly where necessary to help prevent those 'twirly' tangles that look like dreadlocks (Red's and Stanley's particularly do this as they have naturally long soft manes). Both of these things also help prevent twigs and branches getting tangled in their manes and tails too as my boys and girls do like to scratch on trees.

Depending on the conditions over the Winter I might do these things a couple of times and I will sometimes trim fetlocks if they are becoming what I call 'snowballed' with mud.

I do all of these things in the field with the herd as my ponies are used to it and don't blink an eye. As with all activities around your horse – you know them, so be careful introducing new things and allow your horse to 'tell' you when they are comfortable and when they're not.

ONE LAST ACTIVITY
(and this is the most important one)

HAVE FUN!!

Let's face it, being a horse's guardian is costly, time consuming and a huge commitment of sometimes up to 30 something years. Too often this can become a 'slog' or seem to be too hard because of our own and others expectations and the inevitable difficulties that come up along the way. There is also a kind of un-written rule that we must ride our horses "otherwise what's the point?" I hope this collection of alternative activities will show you there are other experiences that we can and should be sharing with our equine family members and this is just the tip of the iceberg!

Once we start to see our horses as friends and partners, rather than a 'tool' or 'piece of equipment' that must be 'used' in a certain way, then and only then can we begin to appreciate and enjoy our horses for who they truly are………fun loving, full of life, wise beyond words, able to live in the moment, deeply loving, loyal, honest and trusting companions that will be there for us when no one else is and who will always know exactly how to make us smile if we just let them.

Have fun…..together…..as friends…..side by side and you will discover what our horses have known all along…..life is for living to its fullest, laughing till your cheeks ache, running like the wind, sleeping deeply, loving fully with compassion, feeling with every sense you have and simply 'being'….now and in this moment.

****

FINAL WORDS…………………………..

So what are you waiting for? Go on, get out there and 'be' with your horse

The great thing about doing these activities is your horses get used to you carrying out different tasks with them and around them, eventually completely at liberty, which is so beneficial in so many ways. Ultimately it means that you won't have to bring your horse in, tie them up, prepare them etc etc, you can simply get on in a relaxed calm way, in an environment your horse is comfortable in and in a way that allows you both to have choices and learn from each other.

THE FREE SPIRIT DREAM……..
Where it started and where we are heading…………..

I wrote this maybe 8 years ago when someone asked me what my dream was…….

This is my dream, this is what The Free Spirit Ponies is - at the moment it's a place in my heart and in the hearts of our herd and animal family but I have a feeling that sometime soon you may be able to find that little battered old sign and come and visit….

FINDING FREE SPIRIT……

Free Spirit Farm is a wonderful place.

It's tucked away down a quiet country lane, set back slightly from the road.

You almost wouldn't know it's there except for the tiny weathered sign hanging, just in the right place; it's metal chain chinking slightly whenever there's a breeze. It hangs from the aged branch of a huge friendly looking oak tree that almost seems to guide you into the small gravel driveway with its strong welcoming branches.

More trees line the short drive to the equally weathered wooden gates which guard the entrance to this little paradise.

On the gate is, what was once, a brightly coloured nameplate, now faded and worn by the years, but somehow warmer and more inviting because of this. It reads "Welcome to Free Spirit Farm – welcome home".

The gravel driveway extends around to the right to an area where you park your car, sheltered by a ramshackle copse of trees and bushes. There are no individual bays or lines or even any signs telling you what to do or where to park but you won't even notice that until you leave and realise it couldn't be any other way.

The entrance gates themselves are tall and solid and very, very old. They look like they would take a great effort to open them but they glide open with a single touch of a tentative fingertip, without a single creak or groan, hinting at the love and compassion that will be found inside.

I would defy even the most hardened and bitter of human being to be unmoved by the scene that fills your senses in that first glimpse of the farm. It is from this moment that you start to see and feel the magic. Instantly you are overcome with the natural beauty of this tiny haven and you become aware that you seem to have left your worries and stresses behind in the car park, although you won't remember doing it.

The strong solid wooden gates close quietly and gracefully behind you and a new world opens up before your eyes.

Just as you think you might just be frozen in the moment, a small black and white cat purrs at your feet and winds itself around and between your legs, begging for a cuddle. This is Patch, the un-official welcoming party, who like everyone and everything else on the farm, does what comes naturally to him. Nobody told him or trained him to do it......he just does.
Once he's said hello, Patch starts to walk towards what seems to be the centre of the farm, urging you to follow with a gently encouraging meow.

On your left is a small thatched cottage, with very well established roses climbing higgledy-piggledy across the front walls. A small wisp of smoke winds slowly out of the chimney and the smell of fresh baked bread fills your nose as you walk past.

The garden which wraps itself around the cottage as if embracing it, is not tidy or ordered – if anything, it is completely the opposite, with far more natural flowers, trees and bushes than any that have been consciously planted there over the years.
There is no pattern or order to the garden except the one that Mother Nature intended. What might have once been a lawn has been decorated in numerous places with splashes of colour from more flowers and bulbs than its possible to count, poking through the rich deep green of the grass, their heads lifted up to smile at the warming sun.

Tucked away under the trailing branches of an enormous willow are two hives, worn so the edges are softened and rounded by years of use and weather; the soft humming of the bees that live there travels gently on the breeze to reach your ears.

Sparrows and starlings flit between the branches of the dark green bushes, carrying food back to their young, tucked away in one of the many hidden and well used nests.

Although the garden is clearly well loved and cared for, it is apparent that it is Mother Nature who decides what flourishes here. It is also obvious that she has a knowledgeable eye because the garden is beautiful and inviting and smells intoxicating.

Just beyond the cottage is another small gate which leads to an orchard and beyond that a large meadow. On the left of the meadow is a huge barn, weathered and ramshackle like everything else.

Everything about its presence, partly tucked away into the woodlands behind, makes you realise it's been here a long time and will be here for a long time to come.

Up until this point it is possible to have not noticed the sounds of the farm, there is so much beauty for the eyes to see and such a peaceful harmonious atmosphere, that you could be mistaken for thinking that it is silent. The truth is that Free Spirit Farm is in fact a very noisy place – it's just that the sounds are all those of nature living and breathing in harmony. These sounds complement each other and are calming and soothing to the human ear - it's just that we, in our busy lives, have forgotten to listen for them.

Along one side of the orchard is a gurgling spring, spurting water from deep in the earth and bubbling down into a small, perfectly formed, stream that runs all of the way around the meadow beyond.

As your eyes follow the journey of the babbling brook, you will start to see the other inhabitants of this little haven. Head bent low, taking a long slow drink from the stream is a sandy coloured pony. Alongside him, a small black and white pig, splashing her nose in the water and rolling around the muddy bank.

As you scan around the meadow and the orchard, suddenly the wonder of the farm becomes clear.

Under the boughs of one of the many apple trees another pig, black this time, sunbathes as a small black and white goat tries to nibble the grass between her ears. Several other ponies are grazing together in the middle of the meadow and tucked between them are three sheep, enthusiastically cropping the bits of grass the ponies are choosing to leave.

There are chickens, ducks and geese everywhere – all colours, shapes and sizes, pecking at the grass; dust-bathing under the trees or simply strutting between the legs of the other animals and you are likely to wonder how you didn't see them before.

Take a walk over to the barn and you will sense the soul of this place; the heart that beats bringing it all together.

There are no pens, no stables, no enclosures or designated areas. The barn is completely open inside and the smell of the fresh, soft straw that carpets the floor is unmistakable and surprisingly welcoming.

Look closer and you will see a small Shetland pony, lying in a corner sleeping peacefully and dreaming deeply. Snuggled between his legs is a pink pig, her head buried in the straw, snoring happily. If you look really closely, you may even see a little foot twitching or an ear flicking as they dream of apples and playing in the sun.

In another corner, several chickens are sitting or choosing where to lay their eggs.

Over to the right, a sheep is feeding her two lambs, while others play in the straw, trying to convince a nearby goat to join in.

Take a step back and allow yourself to see the farm as a whole, living and breathing in harmony and you will become aware that this is a place like no other. Yet it feels absolutely as if this is exactly as it should be; how it's supposed to be – animals, nature and people living as one.

There are no rules and regulations, no bars or cages, no demands or duties, just life at its purest, brightest and most surprising. As you stand and watch, embraced by the safety and comfort of the atmosphere, having completely forgotten the stresses and rigidness of the outside world, you will have a sense of coming home.

I still do every day but I am lucky….because this is my home and I share it with the animals, plants, insects and birds. I experience every day the deep joy of letting go and allowing nature to decide and of being part of her amazing creations.

The front gate is always unlocked.

If you happen to be driving down a quiet country lane this way and you notice a small, weathered sign, hanging from the branch of an old oak tree…..pull in and come and share it with me.

Everyone is welcome.

USEFUL REFERENCES, WEBSITES, BOOKS & OTHER INFORMATION.

If you're looking for a different relationship with your horse, a better relationship based on trust, friendship and mutual understanding and compassion, have a look at our Facebook page The Free Spirit Ponies:

https://www.facebook.com/pages/The-Free-Spirit-Ponies/301243569904837

There you'll find some further resources to get you going, there are many more once you start looking...